Look and Find
Under the Sea

Illustrated by
Gareth Lucas

Designed by Ruth Russell
Written by Kirsteen Robson

The answers are on pages 30–32.

2

I've lost a tooth! Have you seen it?

Where is that carrot? (Maybe it can help me see in the dark.)

16

Look for a compass, lost by a sailor long ago.
Spot someone hunting with a net.
Can you spy a lantern?
Find my remote control so I can swim too!

28

ANSWERS

The striped fish is on page 1.

Cover

1

There are 20 crabs.

2–3

There are 6 flying fish.

4–5

6–7

8–9

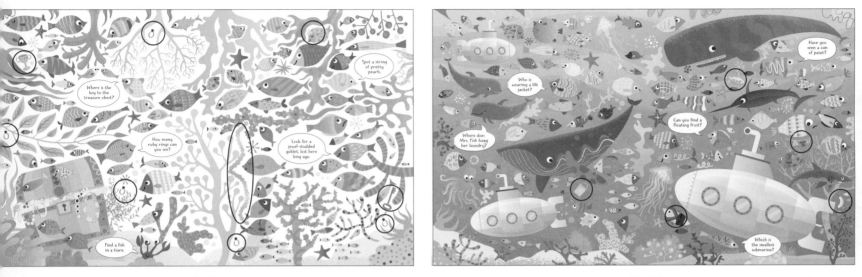

ere are 5 ruby rings.   10-11   12-13

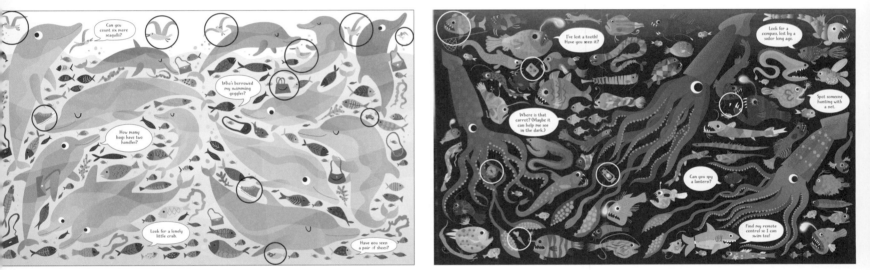

nly 1 bag has two handles.   14-15   16-17

18-19   20-21

ANSWERS (continued)

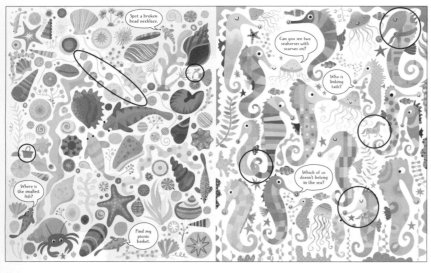

22-23

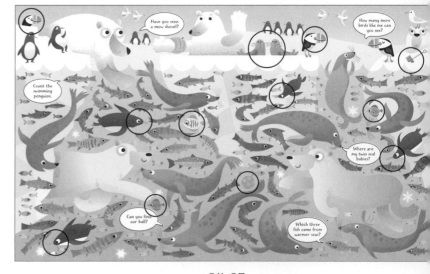

There are 4 swimming penguins...   24-25   ...and 2 more birds like the puffin

26-27

There are 7 more fish.   28-29

This edition first published in 2018 by Usborne Publishing Ltd., Usborne House, 83–85 Saffron Hill, London, EC1N 8RT, United Kingdom. www.usborne.com
Copyright © 2018, 2016 Usborne Publishing Ltd. The name Usborne and the devices ♀ 🎈 are Trade Marks of Usborne Publishing Ltd. All rights reserved.
No part of this publication may be reproduced, stored in a retrieval system, or transmitted in any form or by any means, electronic, mechanical, photocopying, recording or otherwise, without the prior permission of the publisher. UE. Printed in China.